A Prison Camp

Maggie Butt

Maggie Butt

with paintings by George Kenner

Oversteps Books

First published in 2011 by   Oversteps Books Ltd
                                    6 Halwell House
                                    South Pool
                                    Nr Kingsbridge
                                    Devon
                                    TQ7 2RX
                                    UK

www.overstepsbooks.com

Printed in Great Britain by imprint digital, Devon.

Other Poetry by Maggie Butt

Quintana Roo; Acumen Publishing, 2003
Lipstick; Greenwich Exchange, 2007
I am the Sphinx (e-book and mp3); Snakeskin, 2009
petite; Hearing Eye, 2010

Contents

Ally Pally Prison Camp

Alexandra Palace in north London was a WW1 concentration camp for 3,000 civilian internees from 1915 to 1919.
In this book, Maggie Butt's poems are accompanied by extracts from letters and memoirs written by the inmates, and also by photographs and reproductions of a number of George Kenner's paintings of life in the camp. For further information on Ally Pally and its inmates, see notes on page 52 and following.

George Kenner

George Kenner produced the paintings reproduced in this book when he was a prisoner at Alexandra Palace during the first world war. The George Kenner collection can be viewed, by appointment, at the Imperial War Museum, London.

Acknowledgements

Grateful thanks to Christa Bedford, daughter of George Kenner, for permission to use her father's paintings.

Thanks to Nick McCormick, amateur historian; to Katherine Gallagher for her insightful editorial suggestions; and to my friends in the North London Poetry Society Stanza group.

Thanks to the Imperial War Museum for the black and white photographs, Q 64151 / 3 /4 / 5/ 7/ 8, S102, and the letters from which extracts have been taken.

LIST OF ILLUSTRATIONS

First Day Queue

enemy
aliens
single-
file

waiters
bankers
tailors
watchmakers
stock-brokers

tophats
flatcaps
silkscarves
mufflers
frock coats

Savile Row
Sunday best
threadbare
tweed
tatters

suitcase
bundle
basket
pack

pocketed
coppers
photographs
wife
children
letters
papers
wallet

wet
people's
palace
barbed
wire
soldiers
rifles
watching
spitting

silent
shuffle
forwards
officer
names
lists
foreign
Bosch
Hun
signatures
marks

belongings
opened
spread
poked
rain-soaked
stolen

ushered
inside

waiting
waiting
waiting

Otto Weiss – Canary Breeder

I line up in the damping drizzle
under the stares of soldiers,

disgruntled at their back-seat task,
itching to use the friendly bayonet,

feeling through our feet the rumble
of the guns in France, a bass-line

to the songs of birds I name first
in the names my mother taught,

stop guiltily as if the soldiers hear
my thoughts, correct myself: Robin,

Thrush and Wren; wonder who fed
my liebling birds today, lifted covers

from their wicker cages, let their notes
fly out into the room above the shop

as if I almost hear them, gladdening
the morning, pure as water.

The rain comes heavier, trickles
down the back of my neck. The birds

one by one, fall silent.

The Great Hall

The Small Hall

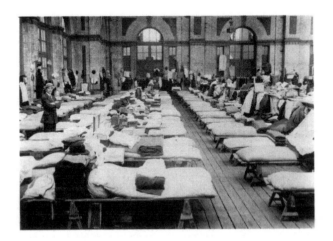

The Great Hall – Battalion B

A thousand iron beds in regimented rows,
each with straw mattress, pillow, blanket,
and a man, entrapped, enwrapped with fear
of how his wife and kids will live.

Beds soon festooned like male harem,
attempt at fabric privacy; draped
too with lively smells of sleeping men,
a thousand snores, a farmyard stench.

Four years of beds so tightly packed
that if he throws out nightmare hand
his wedding ring will clank against his
neighbour's bed, or give him a black eye.

And in the pit of night, sometimes
a guard so overcome by sleep
he drops his rifle with a crash
and wakes a thousand dreaming men.

Dearest Mabel

My dearest Mabel

It seems so long to not know anything about you for almost a week. You can write, but do not exceed two pages. You can send a parcel. I do not need food, we get plenty. Tobacco is the only thing which is always welcome, and send me a reel of best cotton and silk thread.
You can visit but it will be a long way to come for 15 minutes. I am so sorry for poor little Joan. She can't understand why I left her. I met several of my old acquaintances and friends, Mr Rosner is sleeping next to me.
*

We get up at 6am, breakfast at 7am, go out till 12. Dinner at 1, go out till 7, out till 9, bed at 10pm. Every morning, running round the horse race track.
*

I was very much disappointed with your visit. Not with you my dear, but with the time, as I did not know how to divide that 15 minutes between you and Ilona, poor little mite. I have been told she was crying for me when you left. If you can send a little fruit it will be welcome dear. I have borrowed 2/6d. Send it in a registered letter. Days go so slow when I do not hear of you. Some days I have the blues you know. We are only mere numbers here.

Good bye my dearest with fondest love
and lots of kisses to you and the babes.

Benny Cseh
Extracts of letters from August and September 1915

Evenings in the Tower

In the evening we all sit about the tables and by degrees each has, so to speak, become associated with some particular place.

Table one is reserved for readers. At the end of table three you can be sure of finding a game of cards in progress.

Always the same people, playing most noisily, surrounded always by a number of men who never do anything else in the evening but watch the others play.

At the near end people look at newspapers and talk. At table two I usually sit writing; here too sit a pair of chess players and a few others writing.

Next to me on the left sits a man – deprived of his one great joy in life, his glass of beer – who most assiduously and ineffectively tries to learn Russian.

RH Sauter
Extract from letter

The Watch-makers Will Show Us How It's Done

At first the cogs laid out along the bench
the grand and golden, tiny, coppery, dull.

The men who lie on iron beds in private
agonies will start to talk, to work out

who fits where, as minute cogs grow huge
through magnifying eye. In work,

a semblance of normality:
post office, laundry, carpenter's workshop

where a Noah's Ark parade of animals
will march from restless hands

to much-missed children, or for sale.
The pastry-cooks and bakers fire up ovens,

barbers strop their razors, sharpen scissors,
tailors' needles fly. The cogs begin to turn.

This huge machine keeps perfect time.

Early Morning, Post Office, Barbers, Seamen Modeling

Counting-In at 5 o'clock

Paintings by George Kenner

Parcels

My dearest Mabel,

The parcel was in a state. Hardly any grapes was whole, and the plums was in the same way, broken. Only the four pears in decent condition with the tobacco and the silks. Don't send fruits unless very carefully packed. I have received your letter my dear. It was rather long. I'm very sorry Joan do not get better yet. It must be a strain on you. My dear do not give way. You cannot leave a sick child, so don't come. I've been treating myself to a concert in the evening.

*

Two of the pears were in pieces, but the apples were very nice. I have not received the 2/6d yet. I think it is lost. I will be very glad to see you my dear if you think it worth while to come for 15 minutes. It seems I am always unlucky in everything, even in seeing you. Nearly everybody else gets their half hour.

*

I do not want tobacco as I think I will give it up. It is too much to pay 7d now. It was dear before, but I could afford it. But now I do not earn it. I want to try to leave off smoking and you need all what you have at home. Spend it on better food for you and the babes. I hope the kiddies will soon be better. I feel well but I find the time rather long with dreary nights as our room is too dark to read.

Good bye my dearest with fondest love
and lots of kisses to you and the babes.

Benny Cseh
Extracts from letters, October to November 1915

9

Living in The Tower

Out of the flashing sunlight through a narrow passageway and door, so narrow that only one person may pass at a time. And dark. There is a faint gas jet burning. It seems to give no light.

Up 14 bare steps then another nine and still nine more and we are at the entrance of our sanctuary. Now through two solid iron doors, stiff to open, and we are inside that mysterious place, shut off completely from the rest of the camp, whose secrets only a few know.

From the main window the most wonderful view of the distance. The only unbarred window in the tower, and valued accordingly. Out of the windows I get the beautiful views of the palace dome at night.

There is not a single place in the tower through which we cannot catch a river of wind at any moment if we wish.

Imagine the queer and unnatural life that goes on within this ugly and ungainly ark, which from its Ararat looks out over the whole of London.

RH Sauter
Extract from letter

Daily Counting

one
whistle
to get up
stand by your beds
be counted, two or
three times till it tallies

be
counted
again in
the compound, stand
for hours in the sun,
older men often faint

and
after
supper one
last count, and re
count and recount and
recount to three thousand

Kino

Here in the dark, twice weekly transportation,
a long draught of forgetting, the flickering
images so personal we fall head-forwards
into them; that world so wholly lost
where men hop on a bus, clock on at work,
unlock a door and cry 'I'm home' and then
the wonder of a woman's answering voice,
the smell of home-cooked roast.

Our bodies in the Kino seats, our selves
have left to mingle with the crowds
in railway stations, buy a ticket, board
a train, stand on the bows of a great ship
waving a handkerchief, pluck up the nerve
to ask a girl to dance, or roll home singing,
lordly drunk, or cast a fishing line into a river
see midges dance in light upon the water.

We watch with starving eyes the banquet
of free life, the riches of the past
which we once held and spent so carelessly.

The 2/6d

My dearest Mabel,

The 2/6d has been lost my dear. I had a parcel with two cakes and 11 apples quite all right. I earn a few coppers for what I need. It must have been so hard for you to come. Really I do not know how you managed it. I am afraid you worry yourself or overwork yourself. I think you did not look as well as you did before. I am helpless at present. You must act on your own.
*

I am sorry to see that you are getting low spirited. It would be better for you if you could go out more. As to the Christmas pudding my dear, it would be a waste to send it. It would be broken to nothing.
*

Time goes so slowly that I do not know what to do with myself. I did not expect you on Tuesday when I saw the snow. I was in the room only for 10 minutes. I knew you would not come.
*

The free parcel post has been withdrawn. Now you have to pay if you send anything. I do not want anything to be sent. I am sorry to tell you my muffler was stolen last night. I do miss it.

Good bye my dearest with fondest love
and lots of kisses to you and the babes.

Benny Cseh
Extracts from letters, November to December 1915

Rumour

Did you hear? Is it true? Pass it on ...
It was during the raid. (I was under my bed.)
How many escaped? Nobody knows.
It flew them to freedom. Up and away.

It was during the raid. (I was under my bed.)
A moonless night. Our boys know their stuff.
It flew them to freedom. Up and away.
One Zeppelin skimmed the top of our hill.

A moonless night. Our boys know their stuff.
Touched down on the terrace and hauled them aboard.
One Zeppelin skimmed the top of our hill.
Before the guards could lace their boots!

Touched down on the terrace and hauled them aboard.
How many escaped? Nobody knows.
Before the guards could lace their boots!
Did you hear? Is it true? Pass it on ...

Christmas 1915

My dearest Mabel,

I have received the muffler and tobacco today. I wish my dear you were not sending me things. You are more in need. I received the cake yesterday. What does Ilona think about the little chair I made? She seemed to me as if she didn't know me. I wish I could spend Christmas with you. I could put up with quietness after the noise which is going on here all the time.
*

It will be mighty little to live on my dear, it is hard lines, but we cannot help it. You have to sell up and go home. I do not know what else you can do. If you can keep Ilona my dear do not let her go. She is in the best hands with you.
*

The Hungarians gave a supper last night. It was a very nice company of about 42. I had a letter from Nellie and Frank. The 2/6 postal order has arrived. I hope you have spent your Xmas and New Year as cheerful as possible in the circumstances.

Good bye my dearest with fondest love
and lots of kisses to you and the babes.

Benny Cseh
Extract from letter

Making toys

Kitchens – the mid-day meal.

Violinist

My only wife now – see how she trembles
under my fingers, how she fills my days,
demanding more, more, better, better,
no less than my complete compliance.

I'm not a jealous man, I like to share her,
let them admire her voice, the call
of mothers, sweethearts, children,
speaking thoughts we dare not name.

They are hungry for her, twice a week
the concert hall is full for her to sing
the weariness and longing in the hearts
of waiters, tailors, ordinary muted men.

Even the strongest weep with her;
she opens them with skilful surgeon's blade,
lays bare their sorrow,
purifies with flame.

Otto Weiss's Corner

Even in the workshops we can hear them,
over the din of hammer and of saw,
the clear notes of canaries penetrate
like rain through summer shirts.

Waking, he whisks the covers from cages
a cheap magician's trick, abracadabra,
song escapes, cascading through the hall,
rising to the domed glass roof in flight.

Cages of wicker, wire and wood festoon
his corner, hang like fruit in an orchard.
Each of us has dreams of creeping round
at night and setting his birds free.

Visiting Days 1916

It was pathetic to watch the painful excitement of the men whose visitors were due that afternoon: they were a prey to subdued suspense all the morning and as soon as the mid-day meal was over, they started their preparations, each man desperately anxious to look his best.

Long before three o'clock they assembled with their little bundles of flowers and toys for the children, and were then marched off to the visiting rooms, the men sitting at one side of a long table and the visitors filing in to sit down opposite. Here a father with a child on his lap, timidly peering into the face of the strange man, there an elderly couple, hardly speaking just looking and looking at one another with an intensity of longing that words cannot express.

Elegant young women with engagement rings on their fingers, poor working women with a bevy of half starved children, a grim looking solicitor with a pile of papers in front of him – visitors from another world, bringing solace to some and tearing open the wounds of others.

None of the women visitors came empty handed: but their parcels had to pass the censor first and were given to the men when the visits were over. Whilst some of the well-to-do men received huge parcels containing all manners of expensive delicacies, the small packets containing perhaps only a pinch of tea and a diminutive piece of butter, bore eloquent testimony to the self-sacrificing affection in which these poor women held their husbands.

Paul Stoffa
Extract from memoir

19

Visits

Oh! My Darling! Why are people so thoughtless? There seems to have been some muddle about the permit for Mrs H; but even if there was, why could she not write, at least write and let him know how she was getting on?

Since last Monday absolutely no news!
She should have come to see him on Saturday and then on Monday, but both times he hung around the whole afternoon, waiting, waiting, waiting... and afterwards sleepless nights wondering why there was no explanation, why there is no news.

It is not even the 'not coming' – that can be borne, that must be borne – but it's almost criminal to pass over without a single word. That is direct hell for the nerves and leads to endless, tossing nights. There is absolutely no excuse.

It's not the time. To most people time has almost ceased to exist, except for the regular beating of the inevitable food-clock: herring – bacon – nothing; herring – bacon – nothing, and the weekly chime of a short two hour visit to brighten the day.

No, not the time but the waiting, the tension, that nerves cannot stand.

RH Sauter
Extract from letter

The barber's shop

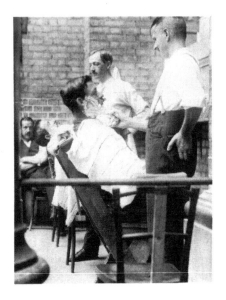

The boating pond

Model Boating Pond

Time flips like a newly landed fish
as you marry the freshly varnished hull
to the buoyancy of water, and are back
when the boat was huge in your hands
and your heart as huge with love for it.

Flip, and you are a prisoner, an alien
in the land where you grew up
and the boat made by your own labour
smelling of balsa and glue,
sails sewn on endless evenings.

Flip as the wind finds sail and the race
begins, with yelling and forgetfulness,
a breezy Sunday afternoon
in boaters and blazers, as if the century
was still new-born and innocent.

Flip and the laughter and the cries
are all of men, no boys – except the boys
inside the men – no running feet,
no women watching as they always do,
just a sentry marking time.

Flip as boats launch from all points
of the compass, taken by the wind,
its helpless prisoners. Only Kurt Engler's
steam-powered tin ship ploughs
its relentless circular course.

The Ballad of Kurt Engler,
Master Hairdresser

His salon was a trip abroad
a place of flirty fun
till local lads broke windows
and painted "Go Home Hun".

Then Special Branch came calling
(and didn't want a trim)
they scrutinised his papers
before arresting him.

They wouldn't drop him off at home
to tell his wife and son
but took him up the Pally –
imprisonment begun.

He set up in the barber's shop
swept up beneath the chair
and fashioned wigs for sale outside
from other prisoners' hair.

Like ancient barber-surgeon
he pulled their teeth as well,
filled dental requisition slips,
discovered he could sell

for quite a tidy profit
something to ease the pain,
for boredom and for loneliness
administered cocaine.

Until the army wondered why
he needed such a store,
extracted his supply chain
and said there'd be no more.

He found the artists' studio
and showed a flair for paint,
his pictures sold like contraband
till guards made a complaint:

he painted future dog-fights
which Germans always won;
his canvasses were gathered up.
No more Victorious Hun.

His missus sold the hairdresser's
and made a little cash,
her letters and her visits stopped.
He worried for his stash.

So chose a moonless, rain-soaked night
when guards stayed by the fire,
threw doubled blanket out across
the walls of looped barbed wire,

rolled on his back to freedom
and stumbled to his feet,
hopped on a passing omnibus,
and rode home to his street.

Banged on the door and shouted
could see the lights inside
his wife just wouldn't answer,
she ran upstairs to hide.

A neighbour came eventually
and told him what he feared:
she'd found a nice new English bloke,
"So go home Hun", she jeered.

Now sodden and despairing
he caught the bus again
returned to Ally Pally's walls
beyond the alien rain.

Censor

Miss Florence Rees's notebook is tight-laced,
hard-backed, she notes in careful hand
(and secret thrill) the covert words a German
spy might use in letters home, heads it
'A List to Watch' and neatly underlines
the clues in camouflage: 'spaghetti' could
mean Zeppelins, and fish like 'sardine'
'tunnyfish' or 'salmon,' disguise armoured
cruisers or torpedoes. Her eyes and finger-tips
are ready to save England, as she feels each page
remembering 'Enemy agents mark their envelopes
with coded pin-pricks'. She takes her work
to heart, and in-between her solid covers
presses wild flowers, a theatre ticket,
a tiny sprig of lavender, tied with ribbon.

Time Do Go Slowly

My dearest Mabel
The parcel was damaged. They are not opened in front of us so I cannot say where is the thief. We can be robbed as we are only Aliens, a so-called enemy. I am considered so dangerous that I am kept here doing nothing while I could earn my and your living doing something useful.
*

We have to stick it my dear. There is no other way. Keep up your spirit for the children. Time do go slowly when I do not hear from you. The children keep getting colds because the house is so draughty. It seems the money goes to people who have money instead to leave it where it is needed.
*

I would be glad now for this life to come to a termination as I get thoroughly sick of it. I am sorry to hear about Mrs Cope's boy. He was a nice boy. The trousers you brought are too short but Frank may be able to use them. Can you get patterns of Donegal tweeds for sporting suits?
*

Lately I have not had much to do. I pass my time in reading Dumas. I am getting sick of this more and more as time goes by. I have no news to tell you. We are in the same old way here, no change of any kind.

Good bye my dearest with fondest love
and lots of kisses to you and the babes.

Benny Cseh
Extracts from letters, January to May 1916

Barbed Wire Disease

The horror of horrors, the one which does not lessen with time but goes on increasing, is that you are never alone.

Not by day, by night, not for a second, day after day, year after year – barbed wire disease – the monstrous, enforced incessant community with no privacy, no possibility of being alone, no possibility of finding quietude.

It is not the men of bad character or morals you begin to hate but the men who draw their soup through their teeth, clean their ears with their fingers at dinner, hiccough unavoidably when they get up from their meal, (a moment awaited with trembling fury by the others), the man who will invariably make the same remark (day after day, year after year) as he sits down, the man who lisps, the man who brags ...

... silly trifles get on your nerves and become unendurable by the simple process of endless repetition.

So grows an atmosphere of mutual dislike, suspiciousness, meanness, hatred. Men become deadly enemies over a piece of bread.

Paul Cohen Portheim
Extract from memoir

Canteen and Stairway to Sleeping Quarters

Wired-off Terrace for Exercise in Bad Weather
For Civilian P.'s of W. near London

Paintings by George Kenner

A Wasted Year

My dearest Mabel,

I feel rather depressed lately. I am very sorry I upset you at your visit. You do not look as you used to, you look much too thin in the face, the result of worry or starving. It seems the letters are more slow lately, it takes a week to come.

**

I am sorry to disappoint you as I see you expected to see me in a better state of mind. I try to smile but it seems too hard at times. I have had no letter from you this week.

**

It will be 12 months away from you by the time you get this.
A wasted year of my life never to return.
Thank you for the butter, milk and cake. It seems to me if
I took it from your mouth.

Good bye my dearest with fondest love
and lots of kisses to you and the babes.

Benny Cseh
Extracts from letters, June to July 1916

Visiting day, August

My beloved soul,

Was it not a wonderful day we held together in the cup of our own hands, when you last pilgrimaged to see me!

And, though we could not have any time alone – did that keep us apart or make any real difference?

All the earth was richly robed in summer, veiled in light – for us.

So my wonderful darling, do not fear, I am not letting myself worry about things, just letting that come which will come and living in the golden hours you bring me.

We must trust to the great unknown to clothe the future in a silver robe.

When one soul lives within the other, then separation loses all its bitterness. Longing will be there, and nothing could prevent that, but for this little time we will try not to let sadness come.

A great message of love I send you, my inspiration, may God bless you a thousand, thousand times until the hour of our reunion.

RH Sauter
Extract from letter, August 1916

The Bromide Boys

The tea tastes strange. They say it's laced
with potions to kill passion.

They leave us letters on our beds
in German, which I cannot read,
from do-good doctor, *hausfrau*, priest
warning against 'perversion'.

As if there were a moment for such privacy.

We amuse ourselves for days
discussing ways to stop the *hausfrau's*
mouth. Crude jokes –
but they remind us we are men.

We look for hair growth on our palms,
our eyesight seems to blur;
we wish we were true monks,
long for absolution.

Killing Time

Who would have guessed its death would be as loud?
That sawing, filing, hammering would mark
the deafening butchery of days?

That minutes must by bayoneted one by one
with noise, in workshops and at bed-sides
carving, beating, pounding, all the daylight hours?

We longed for a quick end to weeks
of grievous separation, swift as pistol shot
or running through with scissored blade,

but every second must be lured, distracted
filled with furious activity before it breathes
its last, bubbling with reluctant blood.

Each morning, after fitful sleep, a new day
to be tortured, poisoned, shaken till its teeth
chatter in its head, driven mad with blasts of noise.

A Nasty Cold

My dearest Mabel,

I feel more cheerful now as things look more hopeful to be with
you in a shorter time. It cannot last much longer.
I wish I could leave this crowd here.
*
I am sorry the house is overrun with mice. If you ask Mr Weiss
to cut you an over coat I could make it here. I am sorry for poor
little Joan. It would be more safe to show her to a doctor.
*
I have had a nasty cold. I got back in bed at 2 o'clock where I am
writing this. I know there is not much prospect even for a fair
Xmas, but try to put up with it my dear. I would be very glad if
you could come early next month.

Good bye my dearest with fondest love
and lots of kisses to you and the babes.

Benny Cseh
Extracts from letters, August to December 1916

It's Just

It's just a cold, dear.
We all have colds.
the laundry flutters with our handkerchiefs
flags of surrender.

It's just a cough, dear.
We all have coughs.
A thousand hacking men who bark
all night, keeping sleep at bay.

Do I look thin, dear?
We all look thin.
The fish is sometimes rotten
and it twists within our guts.

It's just a life, dear.
We all have lives.
Some spill them in the trenches
others in a cage.

It's just a war, dear.
We all have war.

Hungarian Christmas 1916

Christmas Eve – our little club room full of light and colour, a pile of Christmas parcels on the long table, laughter, speeches and above all music.

Our pianist friend poured out a ceaseless stream of Hungarian melodies, some centuries old, unutterably sad, some vibrating with the joy of life.

For a few short hours we were home once more, gone was the War with all its agonies; the world was at peace again and we were free Hungarians in a Free Hungary.

"Lights Out! Come on boys, closing time", booms the jovial voice of the Cockney sergeant at the door.
The lid of the grand piano descends with a slam.

***

Christmas day brought a painful anti-climax to most prisoners; the two hours spent with their families only increased the bitterness of the separation.

Even the Kitchen Committee's supreme effort fell flat: the men did justice to the generous fair, and whiskey, (under the disguise of cold tea) made its way into an endless variety of cups, but all attempts to conjure up the real Christmas spirit were in vain.

Paul Stoffa
Extract from memoir

My first Christmas

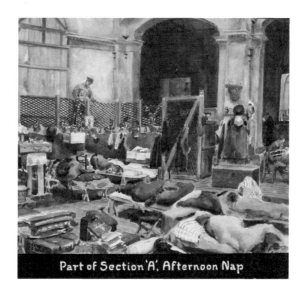

Part of Section 'A', Afternoon Nap

Paintings by George Kenner

Winter

In the summer when the men could go out into the compound things were bearable, but in winter when we had to stay indoors it was hell.

Winter started early that year; the central heating in our battalion quarters wasn't working and we froze in that vast space. Everybody was ill.

The men lay about all day on their plank beds with their blankets over them. Many went down with bronchitis and lung trouble.

The infirmary was filled to suffocation so they had to stay in the battalion quarters. We had a great many cases of insanity.

I had developed chronic stomach trouble and couldn't keep my food down. Not even milk and water. I was no longer the robust man I had been.

It was terrible at night; the coughing and groaning kept us all awake.

Rudolf Rocker
Extract from memoir

From the Sick Bay

My dear little wife

Take many thanks for all you brought me and your dear visit. Sorry I startled you dear one by passing out, but it is nothing so don't worry about it, little woman.

When you come again, don't bring nothing along. No cigarettes. I hardly smoke. So save your little money and buy something for yourself, darling.

Now little feather, how are all the folks? If there should be another year of this captivity there shall be chance of seeing folks at home again.

Well darling, give my love to Eva and Fred, and take my kisses and love from your ever loving husband.

God bless you darling and keep you safe.

Dick Schram
Complete letter, 13th February 1917

(Dick died a few days later)

Alone Despite the Crowd

I have sent Lily's skirts. I am sorry if she is cross, we cannot work here as in a regular shop. I am sorry I forgot about Ilona's birthday. Who would think of her in these great troubles if her father forgot her? She may forgive me when she knows of our misfortune. I hope you are able to get some extra coal to get a little warmth in the rooms.
*

On your next visit you must not bring any food with sugar, flour, jam, syrup milk or cake as they will not be allowed. Mr Bate has left for another camp and I am alone now in spite of the crowd. I will miss him very much. If you can afford my dear get 1½ yard of deck chair canvas. Mr Bate left me his frame.
Joanie was two on Friday and I forgot again. Give her an extra kiss from me.
*

I hope you will be able to get the money. They have no right to withhold it from you. Do not let the babes out of your care altogether, sell out and go home North until better times.

Benny Cseh
Extracts from letters, January to March 1917

The Captured Sailor

Those English fools.
It took them months
to figure out that
though they grabbed me
from a German ship
(money is money
to a seaman) I wasn't
speaking Deutsch,
Turkish or Hungarian.
I sat alone at meals,
walked alone in the
compound because
in all of Ally Pally
not another soul spoke
Welsh.

Tailor's shop

Working the allotments

Allotments

We are peasants, toiling in a book of hours,
four hundred serfs with meagre strips of land
backs bent to digging, weeding, harvesting,
hearts slowed to medieval grace, at last a flowering
acceptance that days will stretch to seasons
whether we rage against our fate, or not.

We count in older ways, a seed for each imprisoned
man; hold conversations about rain and soil,
varieties – the early or the late, a Dutch hoe
or an English; covet seeds like gold in twists
of paper; our cuttings hoarded, traded, swapped;
the land which hates us, blooming in our hands.

We have a purpose now, the slop-free carrying
of cans of water, tucking in the seedlings
watching over them like children. We grow gifts
of vegetables or flowers to give on visit day,
the taste of fresh picked peas, the currency of crops,
the bud and root of unexpected peace.

Doing Nothing

We were quite passive. We suffered in our way but our suffering was of no use to anybody nor were we glorified for it.

We were superfluous, our existence was utterly aimless, our lives perfectly futile, the second great horror of internment life.

One day we were torn from our homes and occupations and put in a cage for no purpose but to wait: months, a year, many years, till the end of our lives, who knew, until war should be over.

There we could do what we pleased, provided it was of no earthly use to anybody.

We lost all count, all sensation of time. Time stands still where there is no aim, no object, no sense. There is no time. One gives in, one surrenders, one's will is broken.

Such monotony is a state very near death.

Paul Cohen Portheim
Extract from memoir

Menu

1915:

The food is good: stewed meat, goulash,
corned beef, pickled or smoked herring.
We can buy cakes, cheese, jam, good butter.

1917:

We haven't had potatoes for nine months
but rice, rice, rice, three times a day,
with swedes and turnips and salt herrings.

Biscuits are broken and full of worms and maggots.
We sent some for analysis but they said
the worms were harmless, we must eat them.

More fights over food than any other cause.

Escape Tunnel

Every prisoner in every cell in every
age and land has dreamed this dream:
a floorboard in the washroom lifts
reveals a tunnel down to freedom.

And this is not a stomach-crawling
earth-in-nostrils, mice and spider
dankness where the earth's weight
groans to bury you alive,

this is engineered, a lofty hoop
of bricks for trains to hurtle through
bringing Sunday-dressed crowds
intent on pleasure at the Pally.

He runs the torch-lit platform length,
kicking up dust, fingers the signs
in their familiar livery, lowers
himself from platform edge to tracks

and walks, upright, with a free man's
heart beating against his ribs, walks
to busy Wood Green station, rides
escalators up into the world.

Alexandra Sports Palace, London, Converted Into Winter Internment Camp 1915-'16

P.o.W. Tailor Work-Shop in Hallway

Paintings by George Kenner

Deported to Holland

Taking leave of my youngster who I might not see for years was especially hard.

On 9th March the camp gave me a send-off. There were tears in many eyes. I begged them not to lose their courage.

When I ended, all rose from their seats and filed past me to press my hand. I had been the focus of all their tragedies and griefs.

Late that night when we lay on our plank beds a sound of singing filled the place. It was a farewell seranade by the camp's choir.

I didn't close my eyes all that night, my last in the camp. My son Rudolf got up to spend the last few hours with me.

He spoke confidently about peace coming soon and of our meeting again, as free men. I tried to hide my fears. I thought of Milly and all my friends and dear ones.

Then I began to wonder what my future would be.

Rudolf Rocker
Extract from memoir, March 1918

Missionaries

A flock of missionaries alights,
black gowned like rooks, to nest
atop of Muswell Hill, a puzzle
to their guards, and to themselves.
Pulling their long beards, practising
the blessing they will rain
upon the heathen – when uncaged
by these other heathen.
Playing cards and singing hymns
to pass the time. Schooling
themselves in patience.

A grave embarrassment –
these men of God seem sent
to undermine the Aliens law,
parading the mystery
of shared beliefs, now
shelved for the duration:

Blessed are the peace makers.

Love they neighbour as thyself.

Turn the other cheek.

Love thine enemy.

Thou shalt not kill.

Nearing the End

These days so filled with great events, just pass us by; here most are in a great state of nerves. Parted from their families, their businesses disappeared as in a quicksand, ill-equipped with energy and health, their faculties stunned by long disuse. These men chose England for their home but it will be impossible to live here afterwards.

Internment does not make such people friendly towards the government; this life has narrowed and embittered us.

But for many Germany is a strange land whose language they do not know and have not learnt in four years of internment. What do you feel is my duty?
What do you feel is best? Should I go straight over to Germany?

You can see the restlessness creeping out: a newspaper picked up, disconsolately, hopelessly to be re-read. A look, a nervous word, a movement of the hand, a conversation which springs up and flickers from mouth to mouth until the whole room is in a blaze of discussion, that inevitable discussion.

For their distraction, people turn to patience everywhere intelligent businessmen, in possession of all their faculties, playing patience at one time, in all corners and tables. It gives one the impression of a mad house.

RH Sauter
Extract from letter, November 6th 1918

Armistice Day

My darling,

Directly after count I walked up and down for an hour and a half, watching the grayness of the day, doing breathing exercises, then worked a little at a watercolour, went to the YMCA for my lesson, for even now life must go on.

Suddenly the guns! the guns!! and one could breathe again.

When the guns slammed out their message at eleven o'clock some men streamed out and shouted, laughing and talking. But many were grave.
The officers have been nice, the soldiers decent.

You dear people! To try to bring me flowers and your little notes. I'm sorry you had to walk so far.
The crowds must have been enormous and the excitement intense – difficult to picture from here where everything was almost deathly quiet.

Oh my darling, you know all my love is near and about you, wherever you are.

RH Sauter
Extract from letter, November 11th 1918

Armistice Conditions

Peace at last darling.

The thought of it is so big.

Armistice – the end of organized murder – this monstrous
bloodshed, this colossal waste!
The useless sacrifices. The waste of it all.

I have just read the armistice conditions and now I see the
real ideals for which the money-grubbing lawyers of the 23
nations have been fighting.

Here one is living among the defeated ... it is upon their
fathers, their mothers, their relatives and friends that these
conditions of slavery have been imposed. The whole of
Germany, one great internment camp.

I see the child of this very day, like a ghost, haunting the
future:

another war.

RH Sauter
Extract from letter, November 11th 1918

Notes

The paintings are by internee George Kenner. George Kennerknecht arrived in the UK from Germany in 1910 at the age of 21 from his home in Munich. He worked in London until 1915, when he was taken to his first internment camp. As a prisoner, he kept a journal, played his violin and drew and painted these atmospheric pictures. He was imprisoned at Alexandra Palace from September 1915 to June 1916, when he was moved to the Isle of Man. More than 100 of his internment pictures survive. After the war he was repatriated to Germany. In 1927, after the death of two of his children in the terrible living conditions of post-war Germany, he took his family to the USA. He worked as a successful commercial artist and died in 1971 at the age of 82.

The camp heroes were prisoner Rudolf Rocker and prison guard Major Mott.

Rudolf Rocker was a famous anarchist and socialist, born in Germany on March 25th, 1875. Scotland Yard called him 'one of the most active anarchists in the country'.
He had settled in London in 1895 to print anarchist propaganda for smuggling into Germany. He was the organiser of the London tailors' strike of 1906, and during the dockers' strike of 1912 he organised Jewish families to feed and clothe 300 of the dockers' children.
He was taken to Alexandra Palace in 1915, where he could be visited by his wife Milly and his eight-year-old son Firmin.
Rocker worked tirelessly to improve standards within the camp and wrote to the neutral Swiss and Swedish embassies about injustices. He was elected 'B Battalion Commander' for the 1,000 men who slept in the Great Hall. His battalion was known as 'the Red company'. He set up a rota for two men to scrub the floor each day. When one man refused to do it, Rocker rolled up his sleeves and did it himself.
Rocker soon persuaded the camp Commandant to relax visiting rules, "I'll see that next time your wife comes to visit you she can hold your hand and you may hold your child in your arms". He knew the greatest enemy was boredom, and he himself delivered 139 lectures during his years at Ally Pally. In June 1917 he delivered his 100th lecture.
In July 1916 his wife Milly was arrested for her socialist activities and work for Russian refugees. No charge was ever

made against Milly but she was kept in Holloway Prison until the end of the war. Their eldest son Rudolf was sent to Alexandra Palace.

By 1918 Rocker was in a poor state: "Worse than my physical illness was my mental depression. All the efforts our friends had made to get Milly released had failed".

Following his deportation, his German citizenship was revoked and he was taken to Holland. He later settled in the US and wrote his book, "Nationalism and Culture" which was known as a classic of libertarian socialism. He died aged 85 in 1958.

Major Mott was the deputy camp Commandant under 'a typical peppery Colonel who had contracted an illness in India and took it out on all of us when he was in pain'. Rudolf Rocker described Major Mott as 'The good angel of Alexandra Palace'. He took charge when the Commandant was ill, saying, "I am sorry for you people. I know what it means to be torn away from your families and your normal life. It is hardest for the older ones. We must do all we can to save them from falling into despair". He acted as defence counsel when prisoners were tried for misdemeanours, including Arndt's extraordinary escape. When Rocker was finally deported, Mott gave his son a job in his office.

First Day p 1

At the outbreak of the First World War in 1914, all German, Austrian and Hungarian men aged between 16 and 42 were required to register with the police. When anti-German riots broke out after the sinking of the Lusitania in 1915, about 42,000 men between the ages of 17 and 55 were rounded up into 'concentration' camps. Those over 55, or invalids, were deported.

Alexandra Palace (known as Ally Pally – the 'people's palace') was a Victorian leisure park in North London which was taken over as an internment camp from 1915 to 1919.

The park at Alexandra Palace was surrounded by belts of barbed wire, with watch towers and 'Tommies with fixed bayonets' patrolling between the wires. The steam pumps for the organ were adapted to run ovens in a cook house behind the orchestra of the Great Hall.

3,000 civilian men (most of whom had English wives) were imprisoned at Ally Pally throughout the war. The Quaker Emergency Committee reported: "The bulk of the men were quiet family men, of good character. Many of them had come to England (or their fathers had) to escape military service or the military atmosphere in Germany. They had looked upon England as a land of justice and freedom, and were genuinely puzzled and oppressed by the sense of the personal injustice that was now their lot".

A further 17,000 men passed through on their way to the other camps throughout the UK. Later in the war these included captured German servicemen, held as prisoners of war.

Otto Weiss p 2

Otto Weiss was a barber who lived and worked in Stoke Newington, London and bred canaries. He had an English wife and an eight-year-old daughter. He was later moved from Alexandra Palace to a camp outside London where his family found it very difficult to visit him.

After the first world war he remained in Britain and became naturalised. In 1938, as another war threatened, a string of mysterious German visitors came to the shop and were ushered into a private room. Otto was later found to have hanged himself. His family believe he was being blackmailed to be a dead letter drop.

The Great Hall p 3

The 3,000 men held at Alexandra Palace were divided into three battalions: A, B, and C. The thousand men of B battalion, under the leadership of Rudolf Rocker, slept in the Great Hall. Each man was given a plank bed with a straw mattress, a straw filled bolster and three horse blankets.

At first they were banned from curtaining off their beds, but later it was tacitly recognised that they needed privacy and were allowed to erect 'four poster' draperies around their beds. Thanks to Rudolf Rocker the initial practice of guards marching up and down all night and 'changing guard' every couple of hours, with much stamping and shouting, which prevented anyone sleeping properly, was stopped and sentries stood watch instead. The lack of privacy and the constant noise had a terrible effect on mental health and a number of men were transferred to the local asylum at Colney Hatch.

English wives and children were also classed as 'enemy aliens'. With their breadwinner in prison, and no Welfare State, many were left virtually destitute. The Quaker Emergency Committee provided tools, benches and timber and bought the goods made in the camps by prisoners and sold them through Friends Meetings nationwide in order to raise money for the wives and children. They took food and clothing to the homes of the wives.

Benny Cseh p 5

Benjamin Cseh was a Hungarian tailor with an English wife and two young children. He was held prisoner at Alexandra Palace from 1915 to 1917. His letters to his wife Mabel are held in the Imperial War Museum. Benny was released from Ally Pally on March 18th 1917 to work in a nursery in Shrewsbury. In January 1919 he was transferred to the prison camp on the Isle of Man where he remained until April, hoping to be allowed to stay in Britain.

Presumably he was allowed to remain, because his daughter Ilona served as a secretary to the US Air Force in Britain in the Second World War.

R H Sauter p 6

Sleeping quarters were issued on a strict class basis.

The labouring classes occupied the Great Hall, the middle classes the Skating Rink, and the aristocracy had quarters in the Tower. As well as beds, the rich had tables at which to sit. The poorer men earned money as their servants.

Rudolf Helmut Sauter was the son of artist George Sauter. He was educated at Harrow School, like his father, and was a fine painter and writer. He was transferred to Alexandra Palace in 1917 at the age of 22, after being held at other camps. Two long letters from him, including drawings, are held at the Imperial War Museum. At Ally Pally he was quartered with the upper classes in the tower.

After the war, his father George returned to Germany, never able to forgive the British government for the internment years. However, Rudolf stayed in England, becoming secretary to his uncle John Galsworthy and illustrating his novels. He lived until 1977, published three books (two poetry collections and a biography of John Galsworthy) and showed his paintings at the Royal Academy, the Paris Salon and widely in the USA. Many of his paintings were destroyed in a fire in 1980, but examples are held in major galleries.

Watchmakers p 7

The middle class civilians held in Ally Pally ranged from stockbrokers and bankers to artists and teachers. Many owned their own businesses. There were also a large number of hairdressers and barbers, watchmakers, bootmakers, tailors, bakers, cooks, waiters and other hotel employees. Some of them were originally toymakers from the Black Forest. At Ally Pally there were workshops for shoe making, glass engraving and carpentry. The products they made were sold by the Society of Friends. There was also a poultry farm.

Kino p 12
The twice-weekly film showings were a highlight of the prisoners' lives. Charlie Chaplin was a particular favourite.

Rumour p 14
Nobody knows whether this Zeppelin escape was wishful thinking on the part of the Germans. Apparently some escaped prisoners made a report about the conditions at Alexandra Palace to the German authorities. They claimed to have escaped during a Zeppelin raid.
The great glass roof of Alexandra Palace was painted green during the war, to make it less of a target during night-time Zeppelin raids. But no doubt the German air force was well aware that the building held imprisoned German nationals.

Violinist p 17
The camp commandant was a music lover and encouraged the prisoners to form an orchestra, Konzert Vereni, which gave concerts on Sunday evenings and sometimes at visit times. Its conductor, Gustave Wanda, had previously conducted at Berlin's Winter Gardens. He became ill and died at Alexandra Palace aged 40.

Visiting, letters and parcels pp 19 and 20
For most of the war, prisoners were allowed twice-weekly visits of half an hour from their wives. However, many wives did not live close enough to be able to take advantage of this and, as can be seen from Benny Cseh's letters, the half-hour rule often became 15 minutes in practice.
The prisoners could write twice a week. Letters had to be in ink and about private and family matters only. Both outgoing and incoming mail was censored (though in May 1916 an officer observed that, as personal interviews were permitted without close surveillance, the postal censorship was near valueless). Benny wrote on standard issue paper, which restricted the length of the letters. Many of his letters are marked 'read by censor'. Harrow-educated R H Sauter wrote on his own paper, letters which extended to many pages.
Benny's letters show that parcels were at first allowed often and post-free. However as the war dragged on, English people were incensed at reports in the right-wing press of German prisoners

living in luxury, so first of all the free post was withdrawn and later a list of 'non permitted' items was issued. Benny Cseh wrote that by the end of the war they were allowed only herrings and apples.

Paul Stoffa p 19
Paul Stoffa was a Major in the Hungarian army who had been posing as a destitute civilian (spying – although he spoke no English) when he was arrested. At first he was put into the Great Hall with B Batallion, "a large airy hall with hundreds of beds neatly arranged, a clean floor and a strong smell of disinfectant, makeshift cupboards containing a queer assortment of odds and ends, faded photographs in shabby frames, tin boxes under the beds. I noticed that most of the men belonged to the labourer class. They had dull, apathetic faces, and the familiar smell of unwashed human bodies and musty clothes". But as he confessed his true identity, he was moved to the Skating Rink and C Batallion, 'the home of the financial aristocracy'. He made strenuous efforts to escape. Eventually he was moved to a camp for Prisoners of War.

Kurt Engler p 23
The details of Kurt Engler's colourful personality and life come from a biography written by his son, Karl Engler, held in the Imperial War Museum.

Censor p 25
Miss Florence Rees's hardback journal is held at the Imperial War Museum. It gives details of the telltale signs of spying, but she also used it to press flowers.
According to Rocker, the censors held letters for two weeks in order to prevent useful information being passed.

Barbed Wire Disease p 27
Camp Vogel or Barbed Wire Disease was a nervous syndrome written up by Swiss embassy doctor A.L. Vischer after the war. Rudolf Rocker described it: "Foremost is an increased irritability, so that the patients cannot stand the slightest opposition and readily fly into a passion. They find intense difficulty concentrating on one particular object; their mode of life becomes unstable and there is a restlessness in all their actions. Failure of memory is a general complaint, especially regarding names of people and places ... Very often people who are affected, brood for three or four days without uttering a

single word. All have in common a dismal outlook and a pessimistic view ... many are inordinately suspicious. I have met with complaints of sleeplessness in a considerable number".

The Bromide Boys p 31
Prisoner Paul Cohen Portheim wrote: "It was rumoured that the tea we got contained bromide intended to calm passion; it certainly had an odd taste". He reported a high level of dirty jokes and talk about sex "which was not more than an outlet for unsatisfiable needs".

He also wrote, "There were certainly a great number of friendly couples considered to belong together". But he did not believe that such close friendships involved sexual acts, partly because there was no possible privacy and also "for many reasons of convention, education and heredity, such homosexuality would not lead to anything approaching sexual intercourse, and would go by the name of friendship, comradeship, mutual sympathy". He notes: "Barbed wire was responsible for an all-pervading atmosphere of hate, but it was also responsible for the birth of a great deal of love".

Killing Time p 32
Paul Stoffa wrote: "The destitute prisoners performed the various fatigue duties, acted as mess-waiters, worked in the laundry and waited on their wealthier comrades. The artisan class was busy in the workshops and the middle-class men devoted most of their time to studies, some to art and music". One of the greatest problems of the camp was the continual noise. Men needed to be occupied and the workshops were not large enough, so they brought their work back to their bedsides, so there was nowhere quiet to read or think.

Rudolf Rocker wrote "The unceasing noise of the camp is a source of constant suffering, which periodically brings men near desperation. It produces a high graded nervousness. I ordered that from 2 to 4pm noisy occupations should cease in B Batallion. But even this small measure failed often owing to the inconsiderateness of single individuals".

For a short while the teachers among the men arranged classes and lecturers and dubbed themselves The University on the Hill, but, as the war dragged on, older men were repatriated to Germany and enthusiasm waned. The YMCA continued to run classes until the end of the war.

Dick Schram p 38

Richard Schram was one of 54 men who died in captivity. This letter was written a few days before his death in 1917 in the Ally Pally hospital. The captured German PoWs who died at Alexandra Palace are commemorated on a stone in a near-by graveyard. Richard Schram is not among them. 23 of the deaths happened at the Colney Hatch Lunatic Asylum.

The Captured Sailor p 40

Paul Stoffa tells the strange story of the Welsh sailor who was captured on a German ship, and held for some time before the guards realised his nationality and released him.

Allotments p 42

400 small garden plots were created for the prisoners. Rudolf Rocker wrote: "No other work had such a beneficial an influence as this. Nothing acts so mildly and so tranquilisingly on the psychological condition of the prisoners as the occupation in the open nature, and though it is not able to resign them to their loss, it helps them greatly to overcome the hopeless creeping monotony of captivity".

Menu p 44

As war dragged on, and food became scarce, the right-wing newspapers carried reports of well fed Germans in the internment camps. In fact, Rudolf Rocker estimates that they got 1,489 calories a day of which 12% was inedible, leaving them 1,311 calories. 75% of the internees fell ill. 500 had ruptures due to constipation. Rocker wrote: "Chronic starvation makes people cowardly and mean; they lose all social sense and become brutalized. They lose hope and become insensible to the things of the mind and spirit".

Escape Tunnel p 45

Rudolf Rocker tells us that beneath Alexandra Palace lay a disused underground station. (Though, curiously, the London Transport Museum has no record of such a station.) Ludolf Arndt volunteered to use its tunnel to take papers from Rudolf Rocker to his anarchist supporters. He was supposed to return the same day, before his disappearance was noticed, but he was held up. Rocker wrote: "keys rattled, doors banged and all the lights went on ... the whole enormous place with over a thousand people rudely awakened from their sleep was like a madhouse ... The Commandant slashed his cane about furiously across Arndt's bed like a madman". He threatened that they'd be kept indoors for 3 days and have no visits or letters for 3 weeks. The Battalion Leaders resigned and the punishment was not carried out. When Arndt returned he was tried and sentenced to 168 days imprisonment with hard labour. Major Mott acted as his defence counsel.

Missionaries p 48
Several George Kenner paintings feature a crowd of missionaries and priests wearing black cassocks and long beards. They had been captured in German Africa.

Nearing the End p 49
The end of the war did not bring an end to internship. Prisoners were still being held at Alexandra Palace well into 1919 while they awaited hearings to decide if they should be repatriated to Germany or allowed to stay in Britain. Even those with English wives and children or business interests were liable to repatriation, which happened with scant warning. Those wives who could get to Alexandra Palace were allowed an emotional fifteen minute farewell. By the end of 1918 21,000 men who were in Britain at the outbreak of war had been repatriated, in addition to 6,800 who were deported during the course of the war. Around 5,000 men applied to stay, and about 4,000 were eventually allowed to remain as 'friendly aliens'.

Bibliography

Letters of internees and photographs held in the Imperial War Museum

Nick McCormick: George Kenner, an illustrated talk. (Bruce Castle Museum)

The Woman's Dreadnought newspaper, ed. Pankhurst, Sylvia

German Prisoners in Great Britain (Tillotson & Son, Bolton and London.)

An Insight into Civilian Internment in Britain During WW1. From the diary of Richard Noschke and a short essay by Rudolf Rocker (Anglo German Family History Society 1998)

Bird, JC: The Control of Enemy Alien Civilians in Great Britain 1914 – 1918 (NY Garland 1986)

Braithwaite-Thomas, Anne: Friends' Emergency Work in England 1914 – 1920 (St Stephen's House)

Carrington, Ron: Alexandra Park and Palace. A History (GLC 1975)

Cesarani, David and Kushner, Tony: The Internment of Aliens in 20th Century Britain (Frank Cass 1993)

Cohen-Portheim, Paul: Time Stood Still. My Internment in England 1914 – 1918 (Duckworth 1931)

Dove, Richard: Totally Un-English? Britain's Internment of Enemy Aliens in Two World Wars (Yearbook of the Research Centre for German & Austrian Exile Studies 2005)

Engler, Karl: Dual Nationality (self published)

Gay, Ken: Palace on the Hill – A History of Alexandra Palace and Park (Hornsey Historical Society. 3rd edition 2005)

Harris, Janet: Alexandra Palace, A Hidden History (Tempus 2005)

Hedgecock, Deborah and Waite, Robert eds: Haringey at War (Tempus 2004)

Mark, Graham: Prisoners of War in British Hands During WW1 – a study of their history, the camps and their mails (Postal History Society)

Panayi, Panikos: The Enemy in Our Midst (Berg 1991)

Rocker, Rudolf: The London Years (Robert Anscombe, London 1956)

Stoffa, Paul: Round the World to Freedom (John Lane 1933)

Vischer, Dr A.L: Barbed Wire Disease (John Bale Sons and Danielson, London 1919)

Other books published by Oversteps

www.overstepsbooks.com